D0918074

SAFETY SAFARI

JoEllen Wilhoite

Illustrated by **Doina Paraschiv**

Best wishes & stay safe!
JoEllen

JOEY BOOKS
Morley, Missouri

An imprint of

P.O. Box 238
Morley, MO 63767
(573) 472-9800
www.acclaimpress.com

Author: JoEllen Wilhoite
Illustrator: Doina Paraschiv

Copyright © 2015
All Rights Reserved.

No part of this book shall be reproduced or transmitted in any form or by any means, electronic or mechanical, including photocopying, recording or by an information or retrieval system, except in the case of brief quotations embodied in articles and reviews, without the prior written consent of the publisher. The scanning, uploading, and distribution of this book via the Internet or via any other means without permission of the publisher is illegal and punishable by law.

Library of Congress Control No.: 2014932722
ISBN-13: 978-1-938905-55-1
ISBN-10: 1-938905-55-5

Second Printing: 2016
Written, Illustrated, Published and Printed in the United States of America
10 9 8 7 6 5 4 3 2

Dedicated to my son and inspiration, Caelin.

*A special thanks to my loving, supportive
and incredibly stable parents, Joseph & Jewell.*

Acknowledgements

My sincere thanks to Amy Riddle, Sam Stephens, Ed McCaw, Jeff Fannin, Elisha Bronston, Carla Mulvaney, Greg Williams, Robert Sarrantonio, Julie Butcher, Karen Murray, Larry Roberts, Michelle Zuck, Neil Chethik, Rayann White, Tammy Waldrop, Rhoda Eldot, Holly Mackley, Ron & Leigh Anne Florence, Bruce Bissmeyer, Gerald Mack, Jan Foody, Robert Stepp, Ronnie Bastin, Derek Anderson, Christopher Hume, Anne Atcher, Tanya Butler, Mollie Dotson, Joe B. Hall, Myra Weathers, Julie Cranfill, Rhenda Kissick, Leigh Ann Guth, Valerie Still, Marsha Irvin, Brant Welch, Maria Holmes, David Bertram, Holly Hopper Dye, Sceane Marshall, Geoffrey Reed, Mike Bosse, Mark Mattmiller, Jack DuArte, Andrea Aispuro, Charlotte Getman, Randy Westbrook, Frank Hall, Charlie Crowe, Carson Evans, Tony Ottiano, Jami Hornbuckle, Jeremy Dixon, Sandra Westerman, Barnes & Noble buddies, Maggie Demaree, Brent Travelsted, and Sean Wilhoite for their support, encouragement, assistance and inspiration.

Ever-growing gratitude to Doina Paraschiv, for her kind spirit, vision, and extraordinary talent and Doug Sikes for believing in my project and facilitating my dream.

Introduction

I have been an advocate for children since I, myself, was a child. I was a sister who defended my younger brother on more than one occasion. Sometimes this required harsh words and other times it required a physical battle. Later, I was a teenager who noticed and took action when other kids were tormented. It was often a helpless feeling to be a child defending and protecting other children. Still, I was willing to stand up to people who were bigger, older and often had more authority than I did.

My own childhood experiences became more relevant after I had my son, Caelin. I started to take, personally, the role that caring adults should have. While he was a baby, I had time to volunteer for the Court Appointed Special Advocate program. Training and association through CASA helped me see the vital needs children have for nurturing, guidance and support.

I wrote Safety Safari because I want children to feel safe and to know how to evaluate and respond to ambiguous situations. Children should know whom to trust and how to find help wherever they may be. I encourage parents/guardians/educators to read through Safety Safari with their children, role play with them, examine the illustrations closely, and help their children practice what to say and how to behave so that they have every advantage when faced with the unknown.

— JoEllen Wilhoite

SAFETY SAFARI

Join safari animals as they lead you through an amazing safety adventure on your quest to become a **SAFETY STAR!**

Have a **SAFE** journey!

Attach your
photo here.

My Current Photo

Include identifying characteristics
such as **age**, **height** and **weight**
on the back of the photo.

To stay safe, it is important to know your entire **name**, your **home phone number** and your **address**. Practice writing them.

Name ___Ollie Elephant___

Address __33 Grass Rd.__

__Savanna, Afri___

Phone # _____

Do you know how to use your home telephone?
Do you know how to use a cell phone?
DIAL 911 IF YOU HAVE A SERIOUS EMERGENCY

Look around you.
Keep your eyes open wide.

Listen to what is happening
around you with big ears.

LOOK, LISTEN, and **LEAD** to be a SAFETY STAR

Lead by taking action to stay safe.

Stay close to your parents in crowded places.

If you get lost in a public place, such as a store or a restaurant, **stand where people can see you.**

Your parents will be looking for you.

Look for a **police officer**, a **store clerk** with a name tag, or **a parent with children** and ask for help. **Wait** with that person until your parents arrive.

Do not leave with anyone!

LOOK, LISTEN, LEAD:

Charlee Cheetah has gotten separated from her mother.
If you were the Cheetah, what would you do?

_____

_____

_____

If you are home alone and answer the phone,
never tell the caller that your parents aren't home.
Say "They are busy."

If you are home alone and someone
comes to your home, **do not answer your door.**

Do not open the door unless **your parents give you
permission** to let a specific person inside.

LOOK, LISTEN, LEAD:

Should the Meerkats open the door?_____
Why?_____

_____

7

Never approach a vehicle for any reason without your parent's permission.

A grown up should not ask you or any child for directions or to help them find something like a pet.

LOOK, LISTEN, LEAD:
What might happen if the Oryx moves closer
to the Nile Crocodile?

_____

_____

_____

Tell your parents, teacher or another trusted adult if someone makes you feel uncomfortable, tries to make you keep a secret or touches your body in places covered by a bathing suit.

If you feel uncomfortable or frightened, you do not have to be polite!

Scream, "No!"
Attract lots of attention.
Run to where people are and tell someone you trust.

LOOK, LISTEN, LEAD:

What could the Vervet Monkey do
to get help from animals close by?

_____

_____

_____

It is safer to be with other people when
you play outside or go somewhere.

Get permission from your parents before
you go anywhere with a person,
even if you know the person.

Make sure you tell your parents where you are going,
who will be with you, and when you will return.

Your parents should be told if any plans change.

LOOK, LISTEN, LEAD:

Is the Lion safer playing in a group?_____

What should the Lion do before it goes somewhere different with this group? _____

_____

13

Internet Safety

While using the internet, the computer, or another electronic device, **<u>never</u> give out identifying or personal information**, such as:

- your address or telephone number
- the name or location of your school
- your parent's work address or telephone number
- pictures of yourself

Sometimes a person might try to trick you on the internet by pretending to be your age when they aren't.

If someone sends you a message that makes you feel uncomfortable or they invite you to meet them, tell your parents or a trusted adult. **Never respond to these messages.**

LOOK, LISTEN, LEAD:

Someone contacts you on the internet and says they go to your school but you don't know them. They ask for your phone number and where you live. What should you do? _____

_____

_____

School Safety

The entrances to your school are locked to keep everyone safe. The school office has to unlock the door to let anyone in during school hours.

Do not open doors to strangers, other students, or even adults you may know.

Tell your teacher if you see anything unusual inside the school or outside the school.

If you see someone who looks or acts strange or scary, tell a teacher.

16

LOOK, LISTEN, LEAD:

You see a strange person hanging around the school playground several days in a row. What should you do? _____

_____

_____

Let a teacher know if another student bothers you or frightens you. If you see a child or adult bothering or hurting another student, you should also tell a teacher.

Be aware of what is happening around you and to the people around you.

Pay close attention to everything you are told to do during safety drills (fire, tornado, earthquake and more) in school so you will be prepared if any of those situations really happen.

LOOK, LISTEN, LEAD:

What should you do during a safety drill?

_____

_____

_____

Home Fire Safety

Create a fire escape plan with your family and practice it.

Find two ways to get out of every room
with your eyes closed. It's dark in a fire.

In Case of a Fire:

Hear the fire alarm? Leave your house quickly!
Fire spreads fast!

Is your door or doorknob hot when you touch it?
Don't open the door! Get out through another door or window.

Crawl to avoid breathing smoke. Smoke
can be more dangerous than flames.

If you catch on fire-**STOP, DROP**
to the ground and **ROLL** back
and forth until the fire is out.

LOOK, LISTEN, LEAD:

Where could your family members meet
outside if there's a fire inside your home?

_____

_____

_____

Tornado Safety

Possible Signs of a Tornado:
- Large Hail • Dark, low-lying clouds
- Dark, greenish-colored sky

Tornadoes make a roaring sound, like a train.

When you are in a building:
Go to the lowest floor level — like a basement. If there is no basement, go to a closet or to a hallway.
*Do not stay inside a trailer/mobile home.
Go to a sturdy building.
Stay away from windows and doors. Protect your head.

When you are outside without shelter:
Run to a ditch or an area lower than the ground. Lie down and cover your head with your hands.

LOOK, LISTEN, LEAD:

The tornado warning is on your television or radio. You should seek shelter immediately. **True or False?** _____

Always remember
to **LOOK, LISTEN,**
and **LEAD** to be a
SAFETY STAR!

I AM A

SAFETY STAR

I Look, Listen, and Lead.

If Your Child Is Missing…

After a thorough search, call your local law enforcement agency. Provide them with the following information:

- ☑ Child's name & nickname
- ☑ Date of birth
- ☑ Height and weight
- ☑ Appearance/identifying characteristics
- ☑ When you noticed your child was missing
- ☑ Who was last with your child
- ☑ Where was your child last seen
- ☑ What your child was last seen wearing

Request your child's name be entered into the National Crime Information Center Missing Person File. Call the National Center for Missing & Exploited Children.

24

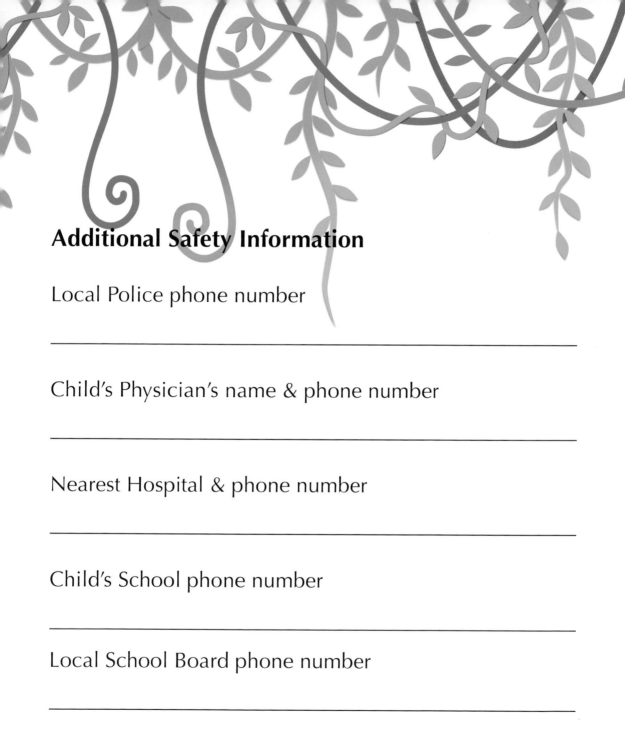

Additional Safety Information

Local Police phone number

_____

Child's Physician's name & phone number

_____

Nearest Hospital & phone number

_____

Child's School phone number

_____

Local School Board phone number

_____

Poison Control Center: **1-800-222-1222**
Call 24 hours a day, 7 days a week

Steps for Obtaining Fingerprints

The child's hand should be washed with soap and water before fingerprinting.

Fingerprinting is easier when your child is standing.

Roll each finger on an ink pad, which can be purchased at any store that sells office supplies. Make sure the entire fingerprint area is evenly covered with ink. The ink should cover from one edge of the nail to the other and from the crease of the first joint to the tip of the finger. It's important to use the correct amount of ink.

Place the side of the child's finger on the accompanying spot on the paw print page. Then roll the finger from nail to nail until it faces the opposite direction. Lift each finger up after rolling to avoid smudging.

Here is My Paw Print

Safety Resources

National Center for Missing & Exploited Children
www.missingkids.com
1-800-THE-LOST
1-800-843-5678

Amber Alert
www.AmberAlert.gov
Used by law enforcement to alert the public when a child is abducted.

The Polly Klaas Foundation
Foundation for the prevention of child abduction, and aid in the search.
www.pollyklaas.org
1-800-587-HELP
1-800-587-4357

National Crime Prevention Council
www.ncpc.org
Helps people keep themselves, their families, and their communities safe from crime.

www.SafeKids.com
Online safety for children

www.netsmartz411.org
Parents' and guardians' online resource for answering questions about internet safety, computers, and the Web.

www.kidshealth.org
Covers information about health, behavior, and development from before birth through the teen years. Four sites in one: with sections for parents, for kids, for teens, and for educators.

www.Ready.gov
Learn to be safe in natural disasters.

Meet the animals:

African Bush Elephant: the largest living land animal; eats herbs and leaves; recognizes its family members .....Pages 1, 4

Mouse Lemur: the smallest primate; nocturnal — which means it is active at night and it sleeps during the day; spends most of its time in trees...Pages 2, 22

Fennec Fox: its large ears can hear prey moving underground; able to live without drinking water, lives on water from food; very social and some people have them as pets .....Pages 2, 22

African Wild Dog: lives and hunts in large packs; chirp and squeak like birds to communicate to each other; endangered —which means there are so few left that they are in danger of no longer existing ....Pages 3, 22

Cheetah: runs faster than any other land animal-up to 75 miles per hour; uses its tail for steering while it runs; hunts by seeing an animal rather than by smelling an animal ..... Page 4

Zebra: each one has its own special pattern of stripes; when chased, runs in a zig-zag, side to side; has excellent eyesight and can see in color .... Page 5

Hippopotamus: can easily outrun a human; very aggressive, one of the most dangerous animals in Africa; most closely related to whales, dolphins, and porpoises .... Page 5

African Lion: sleeps mainly during the day, rests for about 20 hours each day; lionesses (female lions) do most of the hunting; has the loudest roar of any big cat ....Pages 5, 12, 13

Spotted Hyena: can crush bones with its powerful jaws; makes a lot of sounds-whoops, grunts, groans, yells, growls, laughs, whines; born almost fully developed, with its eyes wide open .... Page 5

Rhinoceros: herbivore — which means it only eats plants; nothing in the wild hunts adult rhinos except for humans who hunt the rhino for its horn; horns are made of keratin, the same type of protein that makes up our hair and fingernails; endangered — which means there are so few left that it is in danger of no longer existing ....Pages 5, 20

Meerkat: mainly eats insects but will also eat lizards, snakes, spiders, plants, eggs, small mammals and scorpions; not hurt by certain types of venom (poison), including the very strong venom of scorpions; one of them stands guard while the others hunt for food; makes peeping sounds when all is well but if danger is spotted, it barks or whistles loudly to warn the group........Page 6

Jackal: can run long distances at 10 miles per hour; hunts alone or in pairs; most active when the sun goes down or in the early morning .... Page 7

Nile Crocodile: can hold its breath underwater up to 2 hours; has been around for more than 200 million years; eats everything and can wait for hours, days and weeks for the right time to attack; has the most highly developed brains of all reptiles .... Page 8

Oryx: can survive without water for long periods of time; newborns are able to run immediately after birth; lives in herds of up to 600

Vervet Monkey: spends most of its time in trees; mothers can recognize their babies by a scream; very social and belongs to a well organized group called a troop

African Rock Python: carnivore — which means it only eats meat; kills by constricting (squeezing) its prey; can live up to a year without food if it eats something very large

Martial Eagle: largest eagle in Africa; strong enough to knock an adult man off of his feet; usually only seen in flight.

Parrot: one of the most intelligent birds; can imitate speech and other sounds; uses its feet like hands and its bill (beak) to climb

Tilapia: can only live in warm water; eats weeds and mosquitoes in lakes and rivers; grows very quickly

Piranha: eats meat; has very sharp teeth; lives 25 years

African Hare: can leap 10 feet; nocturnal — which means it is active at night; during the day it spends most of its time hiding

About the Author

JoEllen Wilhoite is a Media Specialist at WDKY-TV/DT. She also works closely with non-profit organizations. In this capacity, she has observed first-hand the need for an instrument to promote safety among children.

While completing her degree at Western Kentucky University, she spent summers providing much needed healthcare to underserved populations. She obtained her degree with majors in Psychology and Sociology and a minor in Criminology.

JoEllen gained business, public relations and advertising experience through work in the horse industry, media advertising and eventually her own advertising agency. She was a Court Appointed Special Advocate, served on the Specialized Alternatives for Families and Youth (SAFY) State Advisory Board, and was a long term member of Bluegrass Crime Stoppers.

Currently, JoEllen resides in Lexington, Kentucky with her son, Caelin, and their dog, Henry.

About the Illustrator

Awards winning illustrator, Doina Paraschiv, was born and educated in Romania. After college, she landed a job with ANIMAFILM, the country's #1 animation studio, where her Art Degree was put to good use. During that time she honed her skills and accumulated an eclectic experience in drawing animation & cartooning. She also discovered how much she loved to illustrate for children...

Now, Doina lives in US with her husband and son. She remains passionate and devoted to her artwork. The artist specializes in children's illustration, and welcomes every opportunity to work with prestigious companies such as Harcourt School Publishers, DIC Animation Studio, and Cabbage Patch Kids, Inc., among many others.